Wildfire

Wildfire

by Patrick Cone

NATURE IN ACTION

Carolrhoda Books, Inc./Minneapolis

For Rhea and Wesley

Special thanks to Wayne Williams, Smokejumper Base, Missoula, Montana, and Jane Kapler Smith, Intermountain Fire Science Laboratory, Missoula, Montana

Text and photographs copyright © 1997 by Patrick Cone, except where noted
Diagrams copyright © 1997 by Carolrhoda Books, Inc.

This book is available in two editions:
Library binding by Carolrhoda Books, Inc.
Soft cover by First Avenue Editions
c/o The Lerner Group
241 First Avenue North
Minneapolis, MN 55401

LIBRARY OF CONGRESS CATALOGING-IN-PUBLICATION DATA

Cone, Patrick
    Wildfire / by Patrick Cone
      p. cm. — (Nature in action)
    Summary: Briefly traces the history of wildfire before going on to discuss types, when and where they start, their behavior, ecological effects, fighting and preventing them.
    ISBN 0-87614-936-0 (lib. bdg.)
    ISBN 1-57505-027-7 (pbk.)
    1. Wildfires—Juvenile literature. 2. Forest fires—Juvenile literature. 3. Wildfires—United States—Juvenile literature.
4. Forest fires—United States—Juvenile literature. [1. Wildfires.
2. Forest fires. 3. Fires.] I. Title. II. Series: Nature in action (Minneapolis, Minn.)
SD421.23.C66 1997
574.5'2642—dc20   95-40847

Manufactured in the United States of America
1 2 3 4 5 6 – JR – 02 01 00 99 98 97

 # Contents

Opening	5
The History of Fire	7
What Is Fire?	10
How Do Wildfires Start?	12
Preheating	14
Flaming Combustion	16
Glowing Combustion	17
When and Where Do Wildfires Start?	18
Types of Wildfire	22
Wildfire Behavior	25
The Ecological Effects of Wildfire	29
Change	29
Regrowth	30
Survival	33
When Are Wildfires Fought?	35
Prescribed Fire	36
Fighting Wildfires	38
Wildfire Safety	43
Fascinating Facts	45
Glossary	46
Index	48

Tall, white storm clouds form high above the mountain peaks throughout the hot afternoon. A few raindrops splat onto the pine needles covering the forest floor. Strong winds rush through the forest, rocking the treetops back and forth. A summer of drought has followed a winter of little snow, and the scene is set for a forest fire.

Jagged, bright strokes of lightning flash from the clouds. Thunder echoes off the rocky cliffs above the trees. With a loud crack, a stroke of lightning hits the top of a tall tree and rips it into flaming bits that drop to the forest floor.

In the twigs and needles beneath the shattered tree, an ember slowly grows into a tiny finger of flame. As the day warms, the fire grows bigger. Then the flames catch a small tree, and before long, the fire spreads high into a tall pine. The tree's dry needles catch fire quickly, and soon the tree is burning like a torch. Neighboring trees start to burn, and smoke fills the air. **Wildfires** are burning in the forest again, just as they have for millions of years.

The History of Fire

Wildfires are uncontrolled fires. They have shaped our planet since the very first plants sprouted. Every area of the world except for moist rain forests and ice-covered lands has a history of wildfire. When the conditions are right, wildfire can burn forests, grasslands, and even marshlands.

But unlike other natural threats, such as floods, hurricanes, and earthquakes, fire is one of humans' oldest tools. Over the past thousands of years, we have learned to use fire for warmth, light, cooking, and even protection from our enemies. Because of its great usefulness, fire has often been treated as a sacred power.

People learned that fire could be a useful tool. Here fire hardens clay pots.

Settlers used blankets, brooms, and buckets of water to fight prairie fires.

In North America, native people used to use fire to shape the land. Their fires thinned trees from forests, which attracted deer, bison, and elk to new grass. They used fires to clear ground for growing berries, grains, and nuts. Native Americans also used fire to drive wild animals toward waiting hunters and to harden clay pots. They sometimes used fire's smoke to keep flies and mosquitoes away.

Europeans brought new sources of wild-fire when they came to America. These new sources of fire moved westward with them. Steam trains shot burning embers into the forests. Miners started fires with explosives. Loggers burned piles of brush. Hunters and trappers often left their camp-fires to burn unattended. During the last century, fires have destroyed logging villages, railroad towns, and mining camps from Maine to Michigan to Montana, killing thousands of people.

Wildfires continue to burn our forests and grasslands. During the dry summer of 1988, lightning caused hundreds of fires throughout the Rocky Mountains. The largest group of these fires swept through Yellowstone National Park. Twenty-five thousand firefighters from across the country and dozens of helicopters and airplanes battled the fires until they finally went out.

The fires of 1988 left behind smoky skies and burned trees. But these and other fires have given hundreds of scientists a chance to study fire, a fascinating part of nature's cycle of life.

The Yellowstone fires burned 793,000 acres in the park and 600,000 acres in the land near the park.

What Is Fire?

We are all familiar with the smell, sound, feel, and sight of something burning. But what exactly is fire? What has to happen for a fire to start? What makes fire burn and grow? And what makes a fire go out?

Fire is a type of chemical reaction, or change from one substance to another substance. Fire is one form of a chemical reaction called **oxidation.** Oxidation takes place when oxygen in the air combines with another material, such as wood or grass.

Fire releases heat, light, carbon dioxide, water, and smoke into the atmosphere. Fire, or **combustion,** is a very violent and rapid form of oxidation. Rusting iron and rotting wood are examples of slower oxidation.

Plants use carbon dioxide from the air, minerals from the ground, sunlight, and water to live and grow. This process is called **photosynthesis.** When plants burn, carbon dioxide, heat, light, and water go back into the atmosphere. Minerals are left behind as ashes and return to the ground.

The minerals left by a fire provide rich soil for new plants.

 # How Do Wildfires Start?

Three things must be present for a fire to start: oxygen, fuel, and heat. These three ingredients make up what is called the **fire triangle.** If any one of these three is missing, a fire will not start.

Oxygen makes up about 21 percent of the air we breathe. A fire simply takes oxygen from the air all around it.

Wood, grass, leaves, pine needles, moss, and paper are all examples of fuel. Dry fuels burn more easily than green or wet fuels. The water in a wet fuel does not allow the fuel to heat up as quickly as a dry fuel. This water also keeps oxygen away.

Fire Triangle

Above left: Dry fuel, such as this grass, burns easily.

Left: In June of 1940, lightning started 1,400 fires in 10 days in the western United States.

Below: Sometimes sparks from downed power lines provide the heat energy for a fire.

Heat is the energy needed to drive water from a fuel to actually start a fire. Lightning is the most common source of heat energy for wildfires around the world. In the western United States, for example, lightning causes 65 percent of wildfires. But many fires are caused by people. In the eastern United States, 90 percent of all wildfires are caused by humans. Sparks from campfires, cigarettes, downed power lines, and chainsaws are some common human sources of heat. Fireworks alone cause nearly 50,000 fires a year in the United States.

Preheating

When oxygen, fuel, and heat meet, the first stage of fire, called **preheating,** can begin. During preheating, the heat source warms the fuel to its **ignition point**—the point at which it catches on fire. The ignition point is different for every type of fuel.

In order for the fuel to reach its ignition point, heat energy must travel from the heat source to the fuel. This transfer of heat can happen in three different ways: by **radiation, convection,** and **conduction.**

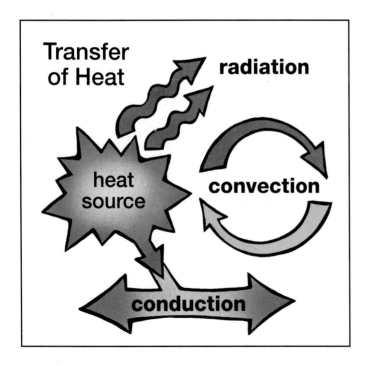

Radiation

Radiation heats a fuel to its ignition point with rays, or waves, from a heat source. If you stand close to a fire and feel its heat, you are being warmed by radiation. We receive our heat from the sun by radiation. Once a wildfire has started, it can continue to dry and preheat the unburned fuel around it by radiation. This keeps the fire burning.

Conduction

Convection heats fuel by the movement of hot air. As air near a heat source warms up, it rises. Cooler air then rushes in to take the place of the rising hot air. The cooler air is then heated, so it rises and is replaced by more cool air. A wood-burning stove heats by convection. As the air around the stove warms and rises, cool air moves in to take its place. Before long, this cycle of moving air can warm the whole room.

If you have ever touched the hot handle of a metal frying pan on a stove, you have experienced conduction. Conduction happens when heat moves through a material. Although the handle of the pan is not over the flame, heat travels through the metal into the handle. Wooden-handled frying pans usually will not burn your hand because wood does not conduct heat well. Fires are not often started by conduction, but fuel can be preheated by conduction once a fire has begun.

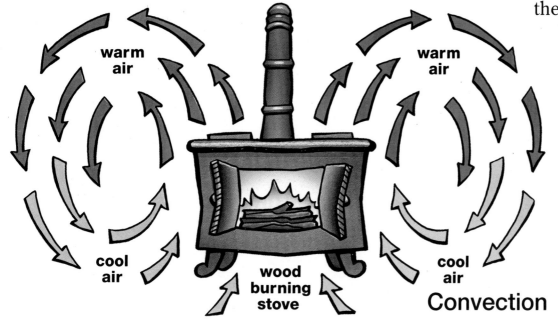

Convection

Flaming Combustion

When the fuel reaches its ignition point, it bursts into flames. The fire has now entered its next stage, called **flaming combustion.** When we think of wildfire, we often think of the spectacular flames of flaming combustion. More heat energy is released during flaming combustion than at any other stage of fire.

Once a fire has truly begun, it needs more and more fuel to continue burning. As the **flaming front,** or burning edge, of a fire enters an unburned area, it preheats fuel by radiation and convection. The wood deep inside trees can be preheated only by the slower process of conduction. For this reason and because there is little oxygen inside a tree, blackened but unburned trees are often left standing when a fast-moving flaming front sweeps through a forested area.

Above right: Flaming combustion

Right: The yellow-orange line of flames is the flaming front of this fire.

Glowing Combustion

After the flaming front passes, fuel burns by **glowing combustion.** During this stage of fire, fuel burns slowly. Red-hot embers can burn for days or weeks after the flaming front has passed through. Combustion stops and the fire finally goes out when the fuel runs out or the oxygen supply is cut off.

Removing any one of the fire triangle's three parts will put out a fire. Firefighters spray water on a fire to cool the heat source and keep oxygen away. They cut down trees or brush in the fire's path to remove fuel. But as long as fuel, oxygen, and heat are present, a wildfire will continue to burn.

Glowing combustion

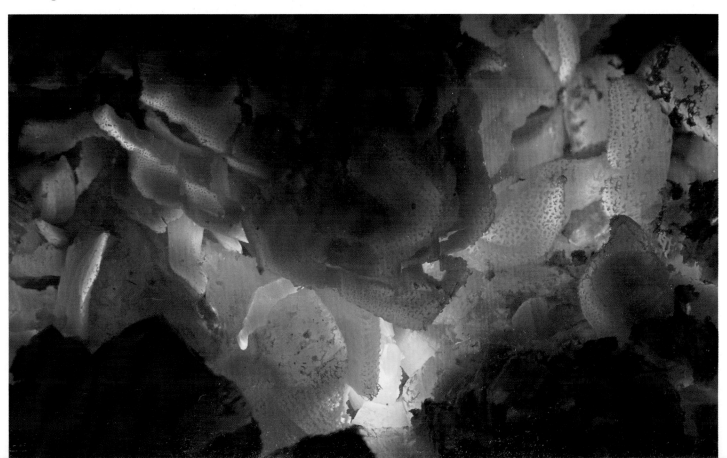

When and Where Do Wildfires Start?

The oak trees and dry grass of southern California *(above)* often burn in the dry winter months. Fire season comes to the forests of Pennsylvania *(below)* in the early spring and again in the fall.

When and where wildfires burn depends largely on **climate,** or the average weather conditions in an area. The temperature, wind, types of plants, and amount of rain or snow are different from place to place. Wildfires burn more often in areas with plenty of plant life (fuel) and at a time of year when there is little rain or snow. Fires are more likely to start during hot weather when fuels are dry than during cool, moist weather.

The time of year in which fires are common is called the **fire season.** Fire seasons vary greatly from place to place. The United States Forest Service lists 15 different fire seasons in North America. Fire seasons depend on the weather and can change each year. Long periods of drought often bring more fires to an area, while unusually wet weather brings fewer fires.

18

Fire season comes to the forested northeastern United States and Canada and to the Appalachian Mountains in the spring after the winter snows have melted and again in the dry, late autumn. In Florida's Everglades and in southern California, wildfires burn most often during the dry winter months. The fire season for the Rocky Mountains and the area to the west of them begins in midsummer when lightning storms ignite the dry forests. Wildfires in the coastal Northwest are uncommon because of fog and rain near the coast and the small number of lightning storms. But wildfires are not unknown in this region—droughts can still produce fires.

Fire in Big Cypress National Preserve, Florida

The amount of lightning in an area makes a difference in where and when wildfires burn. Lightning is the most common cause of wildfire in the world. Across the planet, 44,000 thunderstorms release over 8 million lightning strokes a day. One out of four of these lightning strokes, or 2 million, reaches the ground (the rest travel from cloud to cloud). Only 5 percent of the ground strokes—100,000 strokes—have enough heat to start a fire. A large amount of lightning in an area does not necessarily mean that wildfires will start. Tropical rain forests, for example, have plenty of lightning and fuel, but the wet climate cools the heat and robs the fuel of oxygen.

Cloud-to-cloud and cloud-to-ground lightning strokes

Wind speed and direction also affect an area's fire season. Strong winds feed oxygen to a fire and dry out unburned fuels. Wind also pushes flames toward fuels and preheats them for ignition. Strong winds can quickly turn a small fire into a huge wildfire. Dry desert winds, called **foehn winds,** are some of the most dangerous. The hot Santa Ana winds of southern California are an example of these strong winds. Dry air gains speed and warmth as it drops out of the high desert mountains above Los Angeles. The winds quickly dry the highly flammable manzanita shrubs, tall grass, and oak trees that grow in the region. These winds can turn small fires into fast-moving, dangerous wildfires.

Wildfire destroyed this home and car in Altadena, California, in October of 1993. More than 75 homes burned in this fire.

Types of Wildfire

When fuel ignites, three types of wildfires can result: **ground fires, surface fires,** and **crown fires.** Ground fires burn underneath the layer of dead grass and leaves that covers the ground. These hidden fires burn slowly by glowing combustion and usually go out on their own.

But when fuel is dry, a ground fire can start burning broken branches, grass, and small trees to become a surface fire. A surface fire burns with flaming combustion as its flaming front spreads through fuel. Surface fires clear out dead wood in a forest and burn the **understory,** or the brush and plants near the ground. This cleared forest floor allows a variety of plants to grow. Surface fires usually do not kill the tall trees growing in an area.

If the understory in a forest has not burned for many years, dead wood and short trees can act like a ladder, leading the fire high into the tall trees. When a wildfire travels through the forest canopy, or treetops, it becomes a crown fire, the most destructive and intense of the three types of forest fires.

Above left: A hidden ground fire burned the roots of the pine tree in this photo, causing the tree to fall. **Left:** A surface fire burns the plants near the ground in a forest. **Right:** The flaming treetops of a crown fire can be quite spectacular.

A firestorm in Yellowstone

A fast-moving crown fire skips from tree-top to treetop, sometimes leaving large areas unburned. The most destructive type of crown fire is called a **firestorm.** Firestorms move very slowly or stay in one place and burn nearly everything around them. They can even cause trees to explode like bombs when water deep inside the wood quickly turns to explosive steam from the intense heat. Firestorms release incredible amounts of energy in the form of heat and light. The largest of these destructive fires can release as much energy in 15 minutes as an atomic bomb exploding.

Wildfire Behavior

Once a wildfire has begun, different factors influence the way it behaves. Fuel, wind, temperature, and the shape of the land all affect the actions of the growing blaze. Fuels with natural oils and waxes, such as California's eucalyptus trees and manzanita shrubs, burn hot and fast. Dried grasses also burn fast.

Grass fires can race along at 40 miles per hour when pushed by strong winds.

The type of fuel in an area makes a difference in how forest fires burn. Large crown fires are more common in the evergreen forests of the Rocky Mountains and the Great Lakes states than in the forests of the eastern United States. The dry, oily pine needles of the West are much more flammable than the green, broad leaves of the forests of the Northeast. Northeastern wildfires usually burn as surface fires, clearing the ground for new grasses and shrubs.

Wind and temperature also affect fire behavior. Temperatures usually rise during the afternoons, and so do winds. While high afternoon temperatures and winds dry unburned fuel, winds push flames toward fuel and feed oxygen to the fire. During the night, temperatures and winds generally decrease, and fires usually slow down.

This fire has died down for the night.

26

High winds can also blow sparks and embers far ahead of the flaming front to start new fires. This is called **spotting,** and the new fires are called spot fires. These wind-carried embers can be carried as far as a mile from the fire. In many large fires, spotting has left a pattern of burned and unburned forest.

Large wildfires can even create their own weather. As a large fire heats the air around it by convection, this hot air rises. Cool air rushes to replace the rising hot air, creating a wind that feeds more oxygen to the fire. Hot air and dense plumes of smoke rise high above the fire in what is called a **convective column.** Thunderclouds can even form from the fire's intense heat and send down more lightning that may start new fires.

Above left: While some areas of Yellowstone were completely burned in 1988, other areas were left untouched by fire.

Left: A convective column

Fire burning up the side of a hill. The tornado-like swirl of smoke is caused by the wind.

Landscape can also affect fire behavior. Fires on flat ground either burn fairly evenly on all sides, or they are moved by the wind. But fires in hilly or mountainous areas usually travel uphill. As the hot air from the fire rises up the hill, it preheats unburned fuel further up the slope. Then the fire races up the hill as this preheated fuel bursts into flames.

Sometimes the landscape of an area acts as a natural barrier to a wildfire. With no fuel to burn, rocky cliffs, rivers, and bare mountaintops can keep a wildfire from spreading.

The Ecological Effects of Wildfire

Change

Have you ever seen an area burned by a crown fire? Some blackened trees may be left standing while others may be scattered across the ground. Nothing green and growing seems to be left. Even the ground may be black with ash.

Wildfire can cause major changes to wild areas. Severe wildfire can turn a forested area into grassland. Wildfire can even change the rivers and streams that flow through an area. When the trees, grass, and shrubs that keep soil in place burn, the soil may wash into rivers and streams. After Yellowstone's fires of 1988, four inches of rain fell in 20 minutes and landslides roared down one burned area. Ash and charcoal sometimes cloud the water. This affects fish, insects, and other animals that live in rivers and streams.

Regrowth

An area burned by wildfire may seem destroyed. But look more closely. Even after a crown fire, some grassy meadows and islands of trees were probably untouched. A surface fire might have burned the understory but left trees standing. These trees will thrive without as many other plants on the forest floor. If three or four months have passed since a surface fire burned, you might not even be able to tell that a fire had been there. A variety of new plants may have sprouted in the rich soil left by the fire. Different animals might have moved into the area. In areas where a crown fire has killed the trees, new grasslands or young forests will begin to grow.

New growth covers the ground where a fire burned in Colorado. Notice the pockets of trees left unburned.

Above: The Children's Fire Trail in Yellowstone gives park visitors a tour of regrowth in a burned area.

Right: A flowering plant called fireweed often sprouts after a fire.

Scientists have learned that despite the damage wildfire can cause, fire is an ancient and essential part of a healthy **ecosystem.** In fact, many plants and animals actually need frequent fires to survive. The seeds of the giant sequoia tree in California, for example, grow best in ashy soil. The lodge-pole pine uses fire to survive too. Although lodgepole pines have some cones that drop seeds without heat, they also have cones that open and drop their seeds only when heated to 113°F, usually during a fire. The heat-sensitive cones build up over the years so that when a fire does burn, thousands of new seeds are released. In Yellowstone's lodgepole forests, the wildfires of 1988 produced a new crop of young trees.

A sequoia forest

Survival

When wildfire sweeps through an area, some animals lose their homes, but surprisingly few lose their lives. Small mammals, such as mice and squirrels, can often survive underground until the fire has passed. Birds can usually fly to safety since fires generally burn after their nesting season is over. Large mammals like elk, deer, bear, and bison walk away from the flames and sometimes graze in protected meadows as wildfires roar around them.

The Yellowstone fires of 1988 killed 243 elk, 5 bison, 1 bear, 4 moose, and 4 deer in the park. This is not many compared to the thousands of animals that live in the park. More animals died the winter after the fire from lack of food.

Elk grazing in a smoky meadow

As the snow melted the next spring, Yellowstone came back to life. Seeds sprouted in the rich, ashy soil. New grass, flowers, and berry bushes covered the fire's scars. Birds built nests in the standing dead trees. Grazing animals fed on the lush, new grass. Eventually, aspen trees and lodgepole pines will choke out the smaller plants, as a healthy new forest begins to take over.

Young lodgepole pine trees carpet the ground in Yellowstone. This photograph was taken in 1994, six years after fire burned through this region.

When Are Wildfires Fought?

In the late 1800s and early 1900s, a series of wildfires in the United States burned millions of acres of land and killed many people. After these fires, the modern system of firefighting was organized, and wildfires in the United States were fought whenever possible. Wildfire was seen as harmful to forests and grasslands. But in the 1950s, scientists began to find more and more evidence that fire is important to many ecosystems.

Most wildfires are still fought because they might injure people or damage buildings and property. But scientists now realize that if fires are always fought, dead wood and brush may pile up over the years since it never has a chance to burn. Then when a wildfire starts, it can quickly burn out of control. These large fires can cause harm to buildings and humans, and they are often not as helpful for ecosystems as smaller fires that burn more often.

Prescribed Fire

Wildfires are no longer always put out. A lightning-caused fire in a wildland area that is not threatening anyone may be watched carefully and allowed to burn. This is called a **prescribed fire.** These fires are used to keep wild areas healthy.

The foresters, rangers, and private landowners who manage our forests and grasslands sometimes start prescribed fires on purpose. These controlled fires keep fuels from building up in an area. Natural areas can have the benefits of a fire with little danger of it burning out of control. Prescribed fires are set only when the weather conditions are right, so a large wildfire does not accidentally result.

Dead wood may pile up if fires are always fought.

Yosemite National Park uses prescribed burns. Surface fires are set during moist, windless days to improve the area for wildlife, help the next year's grass, and avoid destructive crown fires. These prescribed fires are started by the same fire crews that fight wildfires. "We're either lighting them or fighting them," says one firefighter. Over 2,500 acres are burned on purpose in Yosemite each year. A prescribed fire costs about $15 per acre, but fighting a wildfire may cost $2,000 per acre.

While prescribed fires and many fires caused by lightning are carefully controlled, most other human-caused fires are fought. Foresters and rangers try to keep these human-caused fires from happening by educating the people who use natural areas.

This forest worker sets a prescribed fire.

Fighting Wildfires

Many people keep an eye on our wildland areas, watching for smoke from lookout towers and airplanes. Fires can sometimes be predicted with special equipment that records lightning touchdowns and weather conditions in remote areas. Once a fire is found, rangers decide whether or not to **extinguish** it, or put it out. Firefighters are called when a fire must be fought. They try to extinguish the fire while it is still small.

To put out a fire, firefighters take away at least one part of the fire triangle. They rob the fire of fuel by clearing a shallow ditch called a **fire line** around its flaming front. Trees, roots, and other burnable fuels must be removed from the fire line, and cliffs, streams, and meadows can be used as natural fire lines. A fire line may be 2 to 10 feet wide if firefighters make it with hand tools, and up to 150 feet wide if bulldozers or power machines are used.

The first fire towers were built by private logging companies. By the mid-1950s, the U.S. Forest Service had built over 5,000 fire towers across the country. Nowadays, most fires are spotted by airplane, and few fire towers are in use.

Left: Clearing a fire line can be backbreaking work.

Above: Fighting a blaze in Utah

Firefighters rob the fire of heat and oxygen by spraying water on the fire from water tanks on their backs or by throwing dirt on the flames.

Fighting fires is a smoky, dirty, exhausting job. Firefighters breathe in smoke and get it in their eyes. They work long hours, sleep when they can, and face many dangers. Wearing lightweight fireproof clothes, boots, hard hats, and gloves, they use chainsaws, shovels, axes, and hoes to dig fire lines. Firefighters work in rain, snow, lightning storms, darkness, and intense heat, all the while keeping an eye out for falling trees, rolling rocks, and wild animals.

Many types of fire crews fight fires. Engine crews drive specially built four-wheel-drive fire engines with large water tanks and high-pressure water nozzles. Firefighters called hotshots travel all over the country, and are usually the first crews on a big fire. Smokejumpers parachute from airplanes to battle wilderness wildfires.

Smokejumpers sometimes fly hundreds of miles to a fire. They jump from airplanes with a total of 75 pounds of equipment, wearing padded suits and helmets with facemasks.

An engine crew in action

Airplanes and helicopters support all of these fire crews. They can find fires, take crews to them, and even help in fighting them. Roaring low and slow, airplanes called air tankers drop **fire retardant** on flames. Fire retardant is a red mixture of water, fertilizer, and sticky gum that slows the spread of fire.

Above: The red color of fire retardant helps airplane pilots see where they dropped it before. Fire retardant has fertilizer in it to help plants grow back after the fire is out.

Below: A helicopter hauls water to a fire.

Helicopters have been used to fight fires since the 1950s. They can drop water on the flames from giant buckets that dangle beneath them. These buckets are often filled with water from nearby lakes and rivers. Helicopters can fly even on windy days, when wildfires are the most dangerous.

Sometimes fire crews fight fire with fire. After fire lines are dug, firefighters set a new fire, called a **backing fire,** inside their fire line. The backing fire and wildfire burn toward each other and meet. With no more fuel left to burn, both fires go out. Conditions for a backing fire must be perfect, or the backing fire itself can burn out of control.

After a flaming front is put out, the slow fire of glowing combustion must be extinguished too. Firefighters have to turn over every piece of wood inside the fire lines. This process is called mopping up. Smoking and glowing embers are smothered with dirt or water so the fire does not begin to burn again. This final operation can take weeks.

Above right: This backing fire (in the front) burns toward the main wildfire, robbing it of fuel.

Right: Firefighters use hoses to mop up a fire.

Wildfire Safety

Even though fires are important to many ecosystems, fires started by human carelessness can harm people and property. You can help prevent fires:

Never leave a campfire or backyard fire unattended. Plan ahead and let the fire die down before you are ready to leave or go inside. Then pour water on the fire, stir the ashes, and add more water. Keep stirring and adding water until all of the burning coals are wet and cold.

Never play with matches. Help keep matches and lighters from young children. They may not know the dangers of fire.

Watch for fire. You can help by reminding adults to be careful with matches, cigarettes, and other fire sources.

Practice safety with fireworks. Many types of fireworks are illegal. Find out what fireworks are legal in your area before using any of them. An adult must be present when fireworks are used, and fireworks should only be started away from anything that could burn.

Know the fire danger in the natural area you are visiting. National parks give a daily fire-danger rating to let visitors know how likely it is that a fire could start. If the rating is high, fires may not be allowed in the area. If a fire starts in a park area while you are there, follow the instructions of the park workers and leave immediately if you are asked to do so.

Report any fires or careless behavior to the nearest fire station or ranger.

For thousands of years, wildfire has shaped our landscape and affected animals, people, and homes. Fire is one of the most powerful natural forces we know—it is both admired and feared by humans.

But we have learned that we need fire to keep our wildlands healthy. Like nature's housekeeper, it clears forest floors and grasslands. Fire releases basic elements that can be used again by all living things. Knowing fire's role in our ecosystem helps us use it wisely and respect it.

Fascinating Facts

In 1871, a wind-driven wildfire roared through the logging and railroad town of Peshtigo, Wisconsin, killing about 1,500 people. Some survived by standing neck-deep in the nearby river with their noses out of the water until the fire had passed.

In 1910, Edward Pulaski hid a fire crew of 45 men inside an Idaho mine while a firestorm raged outside. All but a few of the men survived. In just two days, these fires burned an area 260 miles long and 200 miles wide and left 85 firefighters dead.

The biggest wildfire in possibly the last 300 years burned in 1987. The great Black Dragon fire started in China, where it burned 3,000,000 acres of land and killed 220 people. It moved northward into Siberia (part of the former USSR) where it burned from 9,000,000 to 15,000,000 acres. The total area burned was about the size of Massachusetts, Connecticut, Vermont, and New Hampshire combined.

Fire can lead to disaster, even in the hands of experienced firefighters. In 1989, 7 firefighters were killed in Ontario, Canada, by a prescribed fire they had set themselves, only 10 minutes after they had started it. On July 6, 1994, a fast-moving fire killed 14 firefighters near Glenwood Springs, Colorado. High winds, steep hillsides, and very dry brush contributed to the tragedy.

This fire destroyed Peshtigo, Wisconsin, in 1871.

Glossary

Backing fire: A fire set by firefighters to meet the wildfire and starve it of fuel

Climate: The average weather conditions for an area, including rain, snow, temperature, and wind

Combustion: The burning process known as fire. Combustion gives off heat, light, water, smoke, and gases.

Conduction: The movement of heat through a material

Convection: The movement of heat by hot air

Convective column: A dense plume of hot air, water vapor, and smoke that rises above a fire

Crown fire: A fire that burns the treetops in a forest

Ecosystem: A specific environment and the plants, animals, climate, and geology of that area

Extinguish: To put out a fire

Fire line: A shallow ditch dug by the firefighters to contain a fire

Fire retardant: A red mixture of water, fertilizer, and sticky gum dropped on fires from the air

Fire season: The time of year that fires often burn in an area, due to the climate of that area

Firestorm: A crown fire that stays in one place

Fire triangle: The three ingredients needed for a fire to burn: fuel, heat, and oxygen

Flaming combustion: The stage of fire in which burning gases produce a visible flame

Flaming front: The burning edge of a moving fire

Foehn wind: A hot, dry desert wind

Glowing combustion: The stage of fire in which fuels burn slowly, without a flame

Ground fire: A fire that burns beneath the layer of dead plant material on the ground

Ignition point: The temperature at which a fuel will begin to burn

Oxidation: The kind of chemical reaction that takes place when oxygen combines with a fuel

Photosynthesis: The method plants use to make food out of sunlight and water

Preheating: The stage of fire in which fuel is heated to its ignition point

Prescribed fire: A controlled lightning- or human-started fire that is helpful to an ecosystem

Radiation: The movement of heat by rays or waves

Spotting: When embers are blown ahead of a fire by the wind and start new fires

Surface fire: A fire that burns with a visible flame on the surface of the ground

Understory: The plants that grow beneath the canopy, or treetops, of a forest

Wildfire: An uncontrolled fire

METRIC CONVERSION CHART		
To find measurements that are almost equal		
WHEN YOU KNOW:	MULTIPLY BY:	TO FIND:
inches	2.54	centimeters
feet	30.48	centimeters
miles	1.61	kilometers
acres	0.41	hectares
degrees Fahrenheit	0.56 (after subtracting 32)	degrees Celsius

Thick smoke blocked out the sun during this fire in Yosemite National Park, California.

Index

airplanes, 9, 38, 40, 41
animals, 30, 33, 44

backing fire, 42
Black Dragon fire, 45

change to wild areas, 29–30
climate, 5, 18
combustion, 11; flaming, 16, 23;
    glowing, 17, 22, 42
conduction,14–15, 16
convection, 14–15, 16, 27
convective column, 27
crown fires, 22, 23–24, 26, 29, 30,
    37

ecosystem, 32, 35, 43, 44
embers, 6, 8, 17, 27, 42
engine crews, 40
extinguishing fires, 17, 38–42

fire damage, 21, 35, 45
fire, definition of, 10–11
firefighters, 9, 17, 35, 37, 38–40, 42,
    45
fire lines, 38–39, 42
fire retardant, 40, 41
fire season, 18–19
firestorm, 24, 45
fire triangle, 12, 17, 38
flaming front, 16, 17, 23, 27, 38, 42
forest fires, 5–6, 7, 9, 16, 18–19,
    23–24, 26, 35
fuels, 12–17, 18, 20–21, 22, 25–26,
    38

grass fires, 7, 8, 9, 12, 18, 25, 35
ground fires, 22–23

heat, 12–17, 20, 27, 32, 39
heat, transfer of, 14. See also
    conduction; convection; radiation
helicopters, 9, 40–41
history of wildfire, 7–9
hotshots, 40

ignition point, 14, 16, 21, 22

lightning, 6, 9, 13, 19, 20, 27, 36, 37,
    38

mopping up, 42

oxidation, 10–11
oxygen, 10, 12, 14, 16–17, 20–21,
    26, 27, 39

prairie fires, 8
preheating, 14–15, 16, 21, 28
prescribed fire, 36–37, 45

preventing fires, 43

radiation, 14, 16
regrowth, 30–32, 34

safety, 43
smoke, 8, 27, 42, 47
smokejumpers, 40
stages of fire. See combustion;
    preheating
starting fires, 8–9, 12–15, 16, 20, 36,
    37. See also prescribed fires
surface fires, 22, 26, 30, 37

temperature, 25, 26

United States Forest Service, 18, 38
uses of fire, 7–8

wind, 21, 25, 26–27, 28, 41

Yellowstone fires, 9, 24, 27, 29, 31,
    32, 33–34
Yosemite fires, 37, 47

Additional photos courtesy of: Roger Archibald, pp. 16 (top), 40 (left);
Archives Photos, pp. 7, 21; The Bettmann Archive, p. 8; Corbis-Bettmann,
p. 45; Paul Fieldhouse, pp. 6, 23, 28, 39 (left), 44; Gamma Liaison/Mark
Thiessen, 37; Roger Hungerford, Intermountain Fire Science Laboratory,
p. 22 (top); Diane C. Lyell, pp. 32, 42 (top); Visuals Unlimited/Kirtley-
Perkins, p. 22 (bottom); Visuals Unlimited/Joe McDonald, p. 19; and Visuals
Unlimited/Ted Whittenkraus, p. 17. Illustrations on pages 12, 14, and 15 by
Laura Westlund.